this book belongs to:

for Rufus

This edition published 2008 by Walker Books Ltd
87 Vauxhall Walk, London SE11 5HJ
10 9 8 7 6 5 4 3 2 1
© 1973, 2008 Jan Pieńkowski

The moral rights of the author/illustrator
have been asserted

Printed in China
British Library Cataloguing in Publication Data is available
ISBN 978-1-4063-1437-3
www.walkerbooks.co.uk

WALKER BOOKS
AND SUBSIDIARIES

LONDON · BOSTON · SYDNEY · AUCKLAND

SHAPES

Jan Pieńkowski

circle

square

triangle

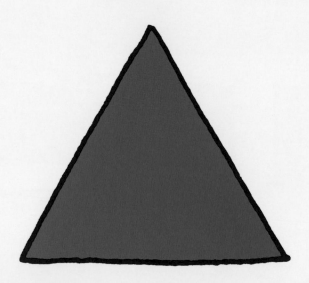

rectangle

oval

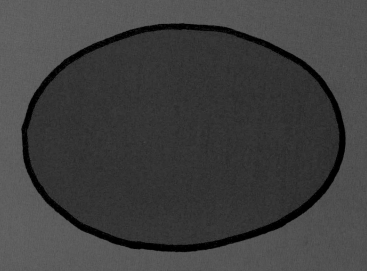

star

crescent

spiral

wave

zigzag

what shape?